Joseph Pergmayr

Meditations on the seven gifts of the Holy Ghost

Joseph Pergmayr

Meditations on the seven gifts of the Holy Ghost

ISBN/EAN: 9783741142277

Manufactured in Europe, USA, Canada, Australia, Japa

Cover: Foto ©Thomas Meinert / pixelio.de

Manufactured and distributed by brebook publishing software
(www.brebook.com)

Joseph Pergmayr

Meditations on the seven gifts of the Holy Ghost

MEDITATIONS
ON
The Seven Gifts of the Holy Ghost.

BY THE
REV. FATHER J. PERGMAYER, S.J.

Translated from the French,
BY E. B. M.

"And the Spirit of the Lord shall rest upon him; the spirit of wisdom, and of understanding, the spirit of counsel, and of fortitude, the spirit of knowledge, and of godliness."—*Isaias* xi. 2.

London:
THOMAS RICHARDSON AND SON,
AND DERBY.
1882.

PREFACE.

By way of preparation to the following meditations, it will be well briefly to explain the various modes in which the Holy Spirit deigns to work in the souls of the children of men.

1. The first working of God the Holy Ghost in the soul is to raise it to a supernatural state. Without this divine operation in the soul of man, it were impossible to please God. It is most necessary, for no one can perform the works of holiness unless God lifts him above the feebleness of nature, and enables him, by this uplifting, to live and act in a supernatural manner.

Such an uplifting is the first operation by which God the Holy Ghost imparts Himself to man. It is effected by means of the Sacraments of Baptism and of Penance. Through these well-springs of grace, the divine Sanctifier frees the soul from the yoke of sin; takes up His abode therein; and enables it, by certain divine gifts, to make itself holy. Man is made a child of God by this indwelling of the Holy Spirit, and is withal endowed with strength and power to lead a supernatural life. This divine working takes place in all just souls,—in children by Baptism, and in penitents when they turn to God by a thorough conversion.

2. The Holy Ghost further works in the soul, and becomes the author of all supernatural actions. Although man is elevated to a supernatural state by the first operation of the Sanctifier, he is, nevertheless, incapable of performing a good deed, unless aided by the renewed influence of this divine Spirit. S. Basil compares man to a ship, which, though excellently built and well equipped for a voyage, can make no way on the waters unless assisted by a favourable wind. In the same way, man, though possessed of sanctifying grace, is unable to perform a single supernatural action, not even devoutly to pronounce the name of Jesus, unless the Holy Ghost pervades the intellect with His light, and powerfully draws the will to union with His own. This influence is of the utmost importance; escape from it would leave the soul barren of all good. S. Cyril of Jerusalem

says: "This Comforter, sent from the Father, is the Guide, the Master, the Sanctifier of souls. All stand in need of His aid; Gabriel and Michael among the angels, Elias and Isaias among men."

3. Now the principal, yea, the only design of the Holy Ghost, in taking up His abode in the soul, is to guide her on the way to holiness. He begins to do this by the aid of Faith, and by means of secret whisperings He breathes into her a spirit of unworldliness, of self-abnegation, of love of God, and of other virtues. As, however, this takes place by the obscure light of faith, and by inner impulses which do not free the heart from the unruliness of sensitive nature, it follows that a soul rarely attains to great holiness so long as the Holy Spirit conducts her only by the path of Faith.

4. The operation of the Holy Ghost in the soul is further carried on by means of His seven gifts. This working differs from the preceding methods. It takes place in the following ways. 1. By an infused light, which points out the truths of Faith. 2. By internal impulses, which move and enlarge the heart. 3. By an inward relish, which lessens, or

takes away, the resistance of corrupt nature, and makes pleasant that which is naturally bitter in the pursuit of virtue. 4. By giving birth to generous and magnanimous sentiments, which exceed the ordinary bounds of virtue, thus exciting the soul to aim at the highest perfection.

"The Seven Gifts of the Holy Ghost," says a holy person, "endow the soul with a certain excellence, and with a promptness in corresponding to grace, enabling her to perform the most perfect and heroic deeds. This excellence consists, chiefly, in a strong interior impulse, proceeding from the Holy Ghost, which breaks down all the barriers to grace, and elicits the activity of the will in the work of perfection. Here, in summary, is explained all that follows. Our purpose, devout reader, is to ponder on the effects produced, by the Uncreated Spirit of God, in the heart of man, and on the happiness which flows into the soul endowed with His seven heavenly Gifts.

The Meditations on the Gifts of the Holy Ghost may be used during the octave of Pentecost, but they will be found profitable at any other time.

Preparation of Heart for the Feast of Pentecost.

In this preparation of heart three points must be considered.

Firstly, what would the life of a devout soul be if deprived of the guidance of the Holy Spirit?

Secondly, the means to be used to the attainment of this grace.

Thirdly, the working of the Holy Spirit in His guidance of souls. This third point has been already spoken of in the Preface.

FIRST MEDITATION.

What would be the life of a devout soul deprived of the guidance of the Holy Spirit? It would be an unillumined life, one without comfort, strength, or energy to take any steps in the way of perfection.

First, it would be an unillumined life. Our Lord compares the soul to a blind man travelling on a dangerous road : he would be in constant peril of meeting with an accident, unless he were led by one who could see. Here is a type of a soul wandering on without the Hand of the Holy Ghost to lead her, for on the road to perfection there are certain paths where it is absolutely necessary to be guided by Him. The conduct of the Apostles SS. James and John is an example of this. They entered once into a Samaritan city with our Lord. The inhabitants received them not, whereupon these two Apostles were filled with indignation, and asked their Master if they should command fire to descend from heaven to consume the inhospitable city. But Jesus rebuked them, saying, "You know not of what spirit you are." But later, when the Paraclete had come, their minds became changed, and they looked upon injuries and persecution as matters of rejoicing. S. Peter wished to deter our Lord from undergoing His Passion; we see him afterwards giving his own life for Christ. The Apostles were ignorant and blind until our Lord sent the Paraclete at Pentecost. Then were they changed;

their eyes were opened to see spiritual things, and their minds were illumined by the Holy Ghost.

It is evident that a soul can do nothing without the aid of the Sanctifier. Did she even possess great virtue, she could make no advance in holiness if the Holy Spirit were to withdraw his illumination. She is like a wanderer in the darkness, bearing a torch in her hands; as long as the torch is alight she walks in safety; should it, however, be extinguished, she is unable to see her way. From these considerations we may gather how necessary is the guidance of the Holy Ghost on the way to perfect holiness.

Secondly, the life of a devout soul, deprived of the guidance of the Divine Spirit, would be a life without comfort. A soul under the direction of the Holy Ghost possesses interior peace, continual gladness, devotion, joy, and fortitude in the practice of virtue. It has been the experience of all God's chosen servants. We read in the life of S. Anthony the Hermit that on his countenance was depicted the inner joy of his holy soul. Compare this happy state with that of one who is not guided by the Spirit of God; such a one is filled with sadness, tepid in prayer, and is troubled when obliged to obey.

Thirdly, a life not guided by the Holy Ghost is devoid of strength or energy to take any steps in the way of perfection. Many people try to obtain some virtue, but they do not seek for the guidance of the Holy Spirit. Our Blessed Lord has said, "I am the Vine, you are the branches; he that abideth in Me and I in him, the same beareth much fruit, for without Me you can do nothing." Thus it is with the soul, as long as she is guided by the Holy Spirit she is ever receiving a fresh supply of grace and of strength to enable her to advance in holiness.

SECOND MEDITATION.

Of the manner in which the soul should prepare herself to receive the light of the Holy Spirit, and the grace to be guided by Him.

There is a vast difference between the life of an ordinary good Christian and that of one who is aiming at perfection.

Much greater preparation is required for the erection of a high tower than for the building of a small house. So also much more care must be taken by one who wishes to raise the edifice of perfection in his soul than what is necessary for another who is living an ordinary good life.

A profound exterior and interior silence is the first preparation demanded by the Holy Ghost of one who is earnestly seeking for His light and guidance.

Exterior silence consists of three things. 1. Silence at all times when it is not lawful to speak. 2. To converse only of praiseworthy things when it is allowable to speak. 3. To keep silence sometimes even when it is not enjoined.

Interior silence requires that we never wilfully entertain a suspicion or rash judgment about our neighbour.

This double silence is necessary for a threefold reason, for as long as it is not observed sin is committed, the virtues of charity, meekness, and humility are wounded, and union with God is impossible. A house with a defective roof, through which the rain can penetrate, is a type of those souls who are careless in maintaining this silence.

The second preparation necessary to obtain the guidance of the Holy Spirit is *perfect submission of judgment and of self-will.*

It is the will of God that man should be governed by man. The Divine Guide never accepts the direction of a soul until she has entirely renounced her own will and judgment. She must be wholly submissive. It would seem that obedience to man is even more pleasing to God than obedience to Himself, for we read in the life of S. Teresa that our Lord in a vision commanded her to found a convent in a certain town. Her provincial, Father Gratian, forbade her to do this. She obeyed him. Our Lord made known to her that she had acted rightly, and He further told her that the foundation should be carried out without her presence being needful.

The third preparation is *constant and fervent prayer.*

The soul that perseveres in these holy dispositions will most surely be purified in time by the Divine Sanctifier, and will be sweetly inebriated with His holy love.

Meditations

ON

THE SEVEN GIFTS OF THE HOLY GHOST.

FIRST MEDITATION.

On the Gift of Holy Fear.

The effects of holy fear are:
1. A profound dread of sin.
2. A detestation of sin.
3. Fear and sorrow for sin solely on God's account.

FIRST POINT.

The thunderbolt, which in a lightning shaft rends the clouds, and breaks upon the dark stilly night with a fearful crash, is a type of that which takes place in the soul before the mighty Spirit of God makes His royal entry therein. His approach is heralded by a sort of lightning flash, which darts through the heart, shedding light where darkness reigned, thus clearly revealing the foulness of sin. The soul is filled with a new and strange sensation. "He looketh upon the earth,"—the heart of man,—" and maketh it tremble." At the coming of the Sanctifier two dispositions are generated in the soul, namely, horror of sin, and great care in avoiding it.

1. As soon as the Divine Spirit bestows the gift of holy fear, a consciousness awakes within the soul, that she is in an altered state. She marvels at the change. Sin is the only evil she now dreads; she shrinks from it with horror. The secret influence which has taken hold of her makes her ready to give up all things, to suffer any torment, yea, death itself, rather than contract the shadow of a stain. S. Catherine of Sienna, deeply penetrated with holy fear, once said, "If on one side I beheld a sea of fire, and on the other the most trivial sin, I should not hesitate to cast myself into the flames rather than commit the sin."

2. These are no empty words, no vain sighs, such as indifferent hearts breathe forth in transient moments of fervour.

Far from it. They are the holy seed produced by the gift of fear, planted in the depths of the heart, which no temptation or unlooked-for chance can uproot. The knowledge which the soul now possesses of the hatefulness of sin, and her resolution of dying rather than offend God, are a sure safeguard in all passing dangers. The salutary guidance of the Holy Spirit renders her firm as a rock in the midst of surging billows. Neither the attractions of the world, the assaults of temptation, nor seductive pleasures, can allure the soul from its allegiance to God. Thus by degrees she frees herself from all defilement of the world or the flesh, and in her victory she becomes like unto the Spouse, of whom it is said by the Holy Ghost, " Thou art all fair, My love, and there is no spot in thee."

How precious is this gift of holy fear. To whom shall I address my petitions to obtain it? Shall I breathe forth my sighs to Thee, O Holy Spirit, who art mercy itself? Or to Thee, O Jesus, who hast so surely promised to send the Comforter as Thy own gift? Shall I turn to thee, O Mary, Bride of the

Spirit, whose every prayer is heard? I beseech of You all to give me a share in this gift. O Holy Spirit, graciously hearken to the sighs of my heart.

SECOND POINT.

The gift of holy fear endows the soul with grace to persevere for a considerable length of time in sinlessness of life, and gives her a love for nothing but the faithful accomplishment of God's will in all that concerns her. Man, however, cannot wholly cast aside the frailty of his nature, and from time to time he falls into lesser faults. Then it is that the effects of holy fear clearly manifest themselves. Her infidelity awakens within the soul a bitter sorrow. She hates herself for it, and seeks, by mortifications, to expiate her offence. Her grief exceeds that of a mother lamenting the death of her first-born. She finds relief in tears, bemoaning her fault, deeming herself worthy of eternal punishment. God alone can give solace to the sorrow-laden soul, He only can wipe away the tears from her eyes. But she is not content with mere weeping; for a slight defilement she condemns herself to penance, which often far outstrips that of the greatest sinners. Alphonsus Rodriguez was an example of this. Every time he passed a certain spot in the house where he dwelt he was wont to cast himself upon his knees, and to beg pardon of God with tears and sighs, reproaching himself with unfeigned marks of sorrow. For many years he acted in this manner. Now, had Rodriguez committed some terrible crime in this place? No; he had been wanting only in custody of the eyes; but by this he believed he had greatly offended his Lord, and in his sorrow he strove to cleanse himself of the stain.

Divine Spirit! my Lord and my God! what impressions ought these truths to make on my mind? Many times in the day I offend Thee, and yet, alas! how insensible I am to my misery. A slight from another, or a harsh word, cause me greater sorrow than a hundred insults which I offer to Thy Majesty. How great is the stubbornness of my will, the blindness of my understanding, and the hardness of my heart. To Thee, O Sanctifier, do I lift my hands and all my heart.

THIRD POINT.

This gift of the Holy Ghost is not a servile fear, but a true filial fear, the fear of loving children. It causes us to hate sin, not on account of the punishment it deserves, but because of the insult it offers to God. Two noble dispositions of heart, imprinted therein by the Holy Ghost, form the groundwork of the gift of holy fear.

1. The first is a profound reverence for the Majesty of God. The soul perceives that His greatness is infinite, boundless, and immeasurable, and therefore we should bear ourselves towards His great Majesty with loving honour and submission. The soul is so enlightened and penetrated with this heavenly light that she counts the sufferings of time and of eternity as nothing in comparison with the hatefulness of the slightest affront offered to Infinite Greatness. She acknowledges that it would be preferable to return to nothingness rather than to offend God by the least sin. As the understanding is con-

vinced of this truth, the will is determined to choose the one before the other.

2. With this reverence for God's Majesty is blended a most tender love. This is the second disposition of filial fear. The soul now is filled with a delicate, sensitive dread of offending God. She would not, by her faithlessness, thwart the love He bears her. She only fears to offend Him, she cares only to belong to Him.

O my God! I have cause indeed to bewail the sad state of my heart. How little am I steeped in holy fear! With what carelessness I offend Thee. Human respect, vanity, and the merest trifles are often the foolish cause of my sins. I am ashamed as I think of my want of sorrow. A thousand venial sins can scarcely draw a sigh from my heart, while a trifling worldly loss fills me with grief. Alas! still sadder is my return to sin after having confessed it, and God has in His sacrament mercifully pardoned me. I am truly in a pitiable state, and the gift of holy fear dwells not in my heart. Take pity on me, O Sanctifier, for if there is a soul more needy of Thy grace than others, it is surely mine. My heart is unstirred by compunction, my efforts to banish sin are but feeble. Come, then, O Holy Ghost, shed Thy light on my understanding, that I may see the hatefulness of sin. Touch my heart with Thy grace, that by its sweet influence I may lament my past transgressions. Inflame my will, so that I may begin at once to destroy and extirpate all that displeases Thee in my heart. The victory of Thy power will be greater in proportion to the change Thou workest in me. Make my heart an abode of holiness. Create, O Divine Spirit, a new heart within me, a heart to choose death rather than sin. Give me a heart which shall grieve only for sin, a heart to fear to displease Thee. Create a clean heart in me, O God, and renew a right spirit within me.

SECOND MEDITATION.

On the Gift of Godliness.

The effects of the gift of Godliness are:
1. Filial subjection to God.
2. Love and benignity towards all creatures.
3. Generous compassion towards God and man.

FIRST POINT.

Many of the difficulties to be met with on the road to holiness arise from hardness of heart. We believe that God is infinitely good, that He is worthy of all our love, that out of loving-kindness He has bestowed upon us all that we have. We acknowledge God to be our last end, and we know that all our joy, all our contentment is to be found solely in the possession and love of Him who is our supreme good. We believe all this, and yet our hearts remain unmoved, barren still of tenderness and love for God. Whence, O my soul, comes this strange perversity? Is it not because the Holy Spirit has not yet come to abide with thee, and the gift of Godliness is not yet thine own? This heaven-sent gift works a marvellous change in the heart. It is like a fire, and works therein the same effects as those which are wrought by material fire on wax. Ponder, O my soul, on this comparison; it is of the Holy Ghost.

1. Under the action of fire wax is so softened, and becomes so pliant, that any impression can readily be made on it. As wax in the hands of the moulder, so does the heart become in the hands of God. He can fashion it as He pleases, imprinting on it the impress of Christ despised and crucified, or that of Christ in the glory of His risen life. David said, "My heart is become like wax, melting in the midst of my bowels." Such a heart is worthy of admiration. It is free from sadness as to the past, without anxiety for the future, in contented restfulness as to the present. It looks up to God with filial tenderness as to a father from whom it has nothing to fear. It is submissive to His will in all things. It blesses and praises Him at all times.

2. Fire again has a still greater power

on wax. It not only softens it, but makes it flow in a liquid stream. The gift of godliness works the same effect in the heart of man. It causes it to flow forth in a spirit of tender devotion and yearning towards God, His honour, and His love. David expresses this in the words, "As wax melteth before the fire." Darkness flees before this heavenly light, troubles vanish, the heart is filled with a delicious peace, and aridity yields to the sweetness of love which flows into the soul. Then are comprehended those words of Solomon in the Book of Wisdom, "Her conversation hath no bitterness, nor her company any tediousness, but joy and gladness."

O Divine Spirit! I lament over the past, for I see how negligent I have been in cultivating the spirit of godliness. Can there be anything more glorious for Thee than to bestow this gift upon us? By it the soul adores Thee in spirit and in truth, she abandons herself wholly to Thy will, she blesses and praises Thee in all Thy decrees, and she rests peacefully under the shadow of Thy protecting wings, which is more precious than the peace, devotion, and love which accompany Thy gift of godliness. How blind I have been. I desire only Thy heaven-sent gift.

SECOND POINT.

The second effect of the gift of godliness is love and benignity towards all creatures. This gives birth to two noble qualities in the soul, qualities which we admire in God's love for us.

1. We acknowledge that God loves all men for His own sake. He regards them as the creatures of His hand, as reflections of His own beauty, ransomed at the price of His Blood, and as sons whom He desires to make co-heirs of His kingdom, so that they may render Him eternal honour and glory. It is for this reason that He loves them as much as His own personal glory, that is to say, in an infinite manner. Love is wedded to godliness. By love we behold God in the person of our neighbour; we love him for God's sake, and we seek God in him. The love which the Holy Ghost inspires is of great tenderness towards God. The affection which we bestow on our brethren for His sake shares in this quality of tenderness.

The love of God and love of our neighbour are so closely united that the one is always found blended with the other. The gift of godliness could not dwell in a heart which had no love to bestow upon the neighbour, albeit it might have some love for God; but it would be a delusive love, or at best a transient waft of sensible devotion, which, passing away, would leave the soul in her former state of weakness.

2. God is not only desirous of doing good to man, but He yearns also to give Himself over to him, and to share with His creatures this eternal happiness. If grief could find its way into the breast of God, nothing would cause Him greater sorrow than to see the obstacles which man is ever putting to the favours which God longs to confer so abundantly. The gift of godliness awakens a similar desire in the soul. She longs to do good to others, she rejoices in spending herself in the service of her neighbour. This longing is so closely united to charity and to godliness, that not unfrequently a greater love for the good of others, more than love of God, is excited in the heart by the Holy Ghost. A

great servant of God, the Blessed Armelle Nicolas, said, "Methinks, O my God, that my love for Thee is less than that which I bear to my fellow-men. My love for Thee makes me weak and languishing, while my love for my neighbour fills me with strength and courage."

Truly, O Divine Spirit, I am a pitiable creature, if Godliness and perfection are manifested in love of our brethren. My misery is twofold, for I do not possess this brotherly love, nor have I sought holiness in the love of others. My heart is not imbued with this heavenly love, for if it were, how could there exist in my mind so many rash judgments, so many suspicious thoughts, or so many other sentiments contrary to charity? I have foolishly thought that the exercises of godliness were to be found in meditation, prayer, obedience, and self-denial. To see and to love God in the person of my neighbour, to rejoice with those who rejoice, to weep with the mourners, to bear with all in silent meekness, returning good for evil,—none of these things, alas! are to be found shedding lustre on my past life.

THIRD POINT.

The third effect of godliness is generous compassion towards God and man. A tender affection for God, and a sincere brotherly love, must necessarily give rise to feelings of compassion, if insult be offered to the one or to the other. This loving sympathy is inherent to the gift of godliness. A pious heart folds within its depths a Christ-like virtue of compassion.

1. Godliness begets compassion towards God. It is true that no creature can do Him harm. He is infinite, and His happiness cannot be increased by the services of His Saints, nor can it be diminished by the outrages of sinners. It is certain, nevertheless, that a devout soul cannot see unmoved the injuries which are being constantly offered to God. Insults offered to a father would wound with sorrow the heart of an affectionate child. The servants of God have felt deeply the sympathy of godliness. Hearken to the chosen soul Armelle: "My Love and my All," she cried,

"Thou hast often wounded my heart so vehemently with the dart of Thy love that it seems to me as if my heart were really pierced. Alas! I have also been wounded by the poisonous shaft of sin. Every time I hear of sin it is like a sword cutting me to pieces, and causing me greater pain than death itself.

2. This gift makes a profound impression on the heart. The tender sympathy which it imprints on the soul, is not merely aroused for the interests of Jesus, it extends also towards our brethren, and causes us to grieve for their misfortunes as if they were our own. Sin causes the greatest grief to those who truly love God. The soul gifted with piety is tranquil and contented. She is a stranger to the outbursts of passion. Contempt or aversion for others never mar her peace. She offers sighs and tears in her efforts to prevent sin; and she has a tender solicitude for the wants of others. This compassion was so manifest in the saints that they seemed entirely to forget themselves in their care for the salvation of souls. "I speak the truth in

Christ," wrote S. Paul, "I lie not, my conscience bearing me witness in the Holy Ghost that I have great sadness, and continual sorrow in my heart. For I wished myself to be an anathema from Christ for my brethren."

O my Jesus, I now understand what the Spirit is which Thou didst promise to send from heaven. It is a spirit of godliness and submission to Thy adorable decrees; a spirit of thanksgiving in the midst of trials. It is the spirit of love and of goodness which transcends all things for the good of others. It is the spirit of sympathy which shares in the adversity or prosperity of others as if they were our own. If this is truly the spirit which is Thy gift, O Jesus, what has filled my heart until now? A mistaken spirit has been mine. A spirit which refuses to believe that sorrow is sent by Thy Fatherly Providence; an unkind spirit, unwilling to help others, yet exacting service from them; an impatient spirit, which cannot brook the slightest contradiction. I see, O Jesus, my shortcomings. I have been swayed by self-love, pride, and caprice. I turn now to the Paraclete

Whom Thou hast sent to dwell among men; He alone can make me holy.

Come, heavenly Spirit, come, and make Thy royal entry into my heart, fill it with Thy own gift of Godliness. Bestow on me a filial love towards Thee, that in Thee I may take all my joy and comfort. Grant that I may humbly adore Thy holy Will alike in adversity as in prosperity. Grant that I may look upon every creature as Thy child, and that charitable behaviour may proceed from all my actions. Breathe into my soul a tender spirit of compassion, so that I may sorrow over the outrages offered to Thy Holiness, and that I may bewail the eternal loss of souls. Weed, O Holy Spirit, from my heart all that displeases Thee, and prepare for Thyself a suitable abode within me.

THIRD MEDITATION.

On the Gift of Knowledge.

The effects of the gift of Knowledge are:
1. Facility in discerning the value of things relating to salvation.
2. Contempt for all that is contrary to God's will.
3. A love of things unworldly.

FIRST POINT.

It is an undeniable fact, that the intellectual blindness which we have inherited from our first parents is a great obstacle to our advance in the way of holiness. We are apt, through this blindness, to set too high a value on the things which are most pernicious to us; and, on the other hand, to despise the very things which are the most salutary. The gift of knowledge alone can rectify the evil. Dwell, O my soul, on the consideration of this divine light, which dissipates the darkness of the understanding, and illuminates the intellect.

1. By a supernatural light the Holy Ghost illumines the reason, and unveils to the eyes of the soul, not only the vanity, but likewise the nothingness and the danger of the world's idols. The soul is then like one to whom sight has been restored. She sees the emptiness of riches, pleasures, and worldly honours. She perceives that all these things can no more content an immortal soul than the air can satisfy a famished beast of burden. She knows that here lies a hidden poison, even as it was found in the forbidden fruit, and as surely will bring forth death. The soul looks on these follies as enemies who would treacherously allure her from her only happiness,—the love of Jesus and familiar intercourse with Him.

2. This supernatural light enables the soul to see the beauty, the greatness, and the profit of those things which the world so carefully shuns. She discovers that amid the darkness of temptation and agony of heart there lies concealed a priceless treasure, to be found only by those who have been illuminated by the

light of knowledge. Adversity, temptation, or grief appear to her now as efficacious means of salvation, as pledges of future glory, and the most precious heritage of the children of God. She fully comprehends the meaning of S. Peter's words, words little understood by the worldly-minded, "If you be reproached for the name of Christ, you shall be blessed; for that which is of the honour, glory, and power of God, and that which is His Spirit, resteth upon you."

I confess, to my shame, O Divine Spirit, that I have but a small share in the gift of the science of the Saints. By Thy mercy I yearn to be made partaker of it. When wilt Thou accomplish my desire, and by the rays of Thy divine light give me to see as clearly as Thy Saints have done?

SECOND POINT.

The second effect of knowledge is a contempt for what is contrary to God's will. This gift not only illuminates the reason with a spiritual discernment of what is just and right, but it also enables the will to choose the right, and to treat with contempt what is contrary thereto.

The operation of this gift is twofold.

1. First, it imparts to the will an aversion for all those things which the world worships. This aversion springs from the inner spiritual light which shows plainly the folly of earthly idols. The soul is like unto a traveller who finds a purse as he wanders on the road at night. The darkness prevents his seeing what it contains, and he imagines that he has found a treasure. With the dawning light he discovers his mistake. The purse is filled only with broken bits of glass, and in disgust he casts it from him. A wanderer in the darkness is a figure of the soul before she has received the gift of knowledge. The goods of this world, its gifts and favours, appear to her as all-desirable; she esteems herself happy if she obtain even a small share of these things. No sooner has the Holy Ghost bestowed the gift of knowledge than all is changed within her. The soul despises what she formerly loved, and is ready to trample under foot those very things which before she took the most delight in.

2. Secondly, knowledge enables the soul to turn aside from worldly vanity. She smiles in secret as she hears others talk of the misery of contempt or adversity. She esteems it a happiness to be despised of the world, and praise only distresses her. With S. Paul she says, "The world is crucified to me, and I to the world;" that is to say, that which the world loves is a cross to her, and that which the world despises is to her a great joy.

How happy, O Sanctifier, are those whom Thou dost deign to instruct. Thou art the Teacher, the Illuminator, and in an instant darkness flees before Thy face. By Thy light the folly of the world is clearly discerned. I beseech Thee, all-powerful Master, to root out of my heart all unquiet passions, and to plant in their stead the seeds of virtue. How happy I should be to be numbered among Thy faithful disciples.

THIRD POINT.

By the gift of knowledge the Holy Spirit not only strips the soul of all affection to earthly things, but He lifts her also to a love for what is contrary to the maxims and wisdom of the world. Man is often as unwise as a child in his choice of moral goods. If a sparkling glass handle and an uncut diamond were offered to a child, he would surely choose the former. Such a choice, however, would never be made by one who knew a diamond's worth. The greater part of men, untaught by knowledge, act in a like childish fashion where spiritual goods are concerned, but an enlightened soul estimates them at their real value. What aforetime she sought after now she despises. Knowledge has given her a taste for things which are grievous to corrupt nature.

2. From the inflowing of the gift of knowledge saintly desires and generous aspirations stream through the heart. The soul, in love with suffering, asks of our Lord to give her Himself as the only requital she yearns after for fidelity in His service. Jesus asked S. John of the Cross in what manner he desired to be rewarded. The Saint replied, "My Lord and my God, I desire to suffer and to be despised for love for Thee."

I implore of Thee, O Divine Spirit, to cast Thine eyes on Thy miserable servant. I see the wretchedness of my heart by the light of Thy truth. I acknowledge that worldly honours and pleasures are as nothingness before Thee. Thou hast made known to me the value of those things which are foolishness to the world. I see how helpful they may be on the road to holiness. Faith teaches me this, yet no change is wrought in my heart. I still love as the world loves, and hate as it hates. Take pity, then, on me. Delay not in Thy coming, for Thou only canst change me. Come and illuminate me with Thy light, inflame me with Thy love. One ray will suffice to quicken my intellect, one spark of the holy flame will set my will on fire. Give me a share in the science of the Saints. They only desired to be conformed to the likeness of Christ crucified. Thou canst fashion my heart after the same pattern. Thou hast but to will it, and immediately I shall love as the Saints loved. My heart is ready, O God, it sighs for Thee to come and fill it.

FOURTH MEDITATION,

On the Gift of Fortitude.

The effects of the gift of Fortitude are:
1. Courage in the execution of good resolutions.
2. Endurance in the hour of temptation.
3. Calm inflexibility in trouble.

FIRST POINT.

Nothing costs so little as the framing of good resolutions. Even tepid souls are not slow in this matter after attending for a short time to some devout exercise. Acceptance of suffering, self-renouncement, obedience, and patience, are among the virtues which they determine to practise. If all good purposes were faithfully kept, Convents would speedily be filled with Saints. Experience, however, teaches that it is a rare thing to find souls who carry out their pious resolutions. Natural feebleness and inconstancy soon get the upper hand, and the performance of resolves made in fervorous moments seems to be beyond our strength. Be not discouraged, O my soul, it is in the power of the Holy Ghost to strengthen thee. He can give thee to overcome all weakness. Learn in what manner He will do so.

1. It sometimes happens that the Sanctifier, in taking entire possession of a soul, withdraws from it all natural repugnance. He establishes within the heart inward peace, and enkindles so ardent a fire of love that the soul desires nothing but to become well-pleasing to her Beloved. She surrenders herself to His sway, and she uses her best endeavours to exercise herself in virtue. She hearkens to no cry of sensitive nature, she heeds no sting of pain. Love makes all things easy, and the soul feels ready to shed her blood for Christ's dear sake.

2. The Holy Spirit does not, however, draw all souls to Himself in this manner. He permits some to undergo the most dreadful combats; nature revolts, and the attainment of holiness appears well-nigh impossible. The Divine Sanctifier, meanwhile, is not unmindful of His

servant. He sanctions these interior struggles, but at the same time He animates her to resistance, and enables her by secret impulses to attack the enemy with valour. Then the revolt of nature becomes a trial no longer; the soul takes therein a secret joy, for it gives her an opportunity of proving her fidelity and love to Jesus. By degrees, as she grows more courageous, she takes absolute pleasure in self-subjugation, and is anxious to fight still longer for Christ.

I perceive, O Holy Spirit, whence arose my inconstancy and weakness. I have not yet received the gift of fortitude. I must blame myself, for, in my self-confidence, I have not called on Thee for help in the hour of trial. I have been indifferent to Thy gift, and I have not pleaded for it; thus I was easily vanquished by the tempter. What reason have I not to bewail the past!

SECOND POINT.

Fortitude is of the utmost importance in the perilous time of temptation, especially when, in order to purify her, and to make her meet for union with Himself, God allows the soul to be set up as a mark for the fury of the evil one. Hell itself seems determined to effect her ruin. Day and night she is a prey to the most vehement temptation; it seems to her that she must yield to the seduction. Darkness is around her, and, unable to render an account of what is passing within her, the soul feels she can hold out no longer, and she must die of sorrow. Fortitude then comes forth to perfect the will. The operation of the Holy Ghost in this gift is twofold.

1. The first working is of so subtle a nature that the soul is at first unconscious of it. There is enacted in the heart a scene similar to that which took place one day in the Apostles' bark on the Galilean sea. There came a storm of wind, and the waves beat into the ship, so that the ship was filled. Jesus was asleep, apparently unmindful of the danger they were in, yet His Heart was watching, and by His omnipotence He stilled the angry storm. Thus does the Holy Spirit act in the soul in temptation's hour. She becomes, as it were, the sport of the devil, and she sees no means of escape from the threatening danger. The Holy Ghost appears to

sleep, but in reality He is watching in the depths of the heart, and gives to the soul a secret strength by which she remains invincible. She is as safe as Jonas was in the jaws of the whale, protected by the hand of God.

2. Through the second working the Sanctifier gives more perceptible help. He shows Himself in the midst of the tempest, breathing peace around, and endows the soul with such a mighty strength, that, like S. Anthony, she is enabled to scoff at the spirits of evil. "The love of God," said Armelle Nicolas, "was like a fire which overthrew all the obstacles which came in its way. This love gave birth in my heart to so great a strength, that if I had been surrounded by all the powers of hell, they could not have done me the least harm. This strength increased with the assaults of the tempter. Oftentimes, when I feared he was about to become victor, I suddenly felt a great increase of inward power. Then, in contempt, I defied him to hurt me, and he fled away in terror."

When shall I be made partaker of this grace, so that temptation will cause me no more alarm, and I shall be enabled to scorn even the evil one himself? Until now, O Holy Spirit, his least attack has affrighted me, for I was not only in danger of losing peace of soul, but I was in constant fear of defeat. How necessary it is for me to turn to Thee! How needful is Thy gracious assistance!

THIRD POINT.

The third effect of fortitude is a calm inflexibility in the midst of trouble. In the hour of trial we are liable to fall into two evils, excessive grief, and inordinate desire to be freed from our sorrow. The Holy Ghost guards us from these evils by the gift of fortitude.

1. Fortitude removes excessive grief, and implants in its place a holy joy. Grace is, we know, all-powerful, and yet, can it breed within the heart consolation in the midst of bitter sorrow? We see that this is the case in purgatory. The holy souls are content in the consuming flames. "It is impossible to say," said the learned Louis Da Ponte, "if the pains of the souls in purgatory surpass their joy, or if, on the contrary, their exceeding consolation does not far outstrip

their suffering." The operation of the Holy Spirit amid the blessed captives finds its place, likewise, in the heart of man. A soul in whom He abides is not callous to grief: it is as bitter to her as to others, but with it is blended a holy joy, and it is difficult to say which is the greater, the grief or the joy. The desire of pleasing God, and to be crucified in spirit with Jesus, makes the cross dear to the soul; burning with the flames of love, she is inundated with a heavenly contentment, though she may be steeped in suffering. S. Paul tells us that he was filled with joy in the midst of tribulation.

2. The Holy Spirit withdraws from the heart of His faithful servants all desire to be freed from trials. At the same time He bestows a great love of suffering. This second working is the consequence of the preceding one. For as the soul takes joy in tribulation, so her love for it grows stronger. She desires to cling to the cross until God calls her to Himself. "To suffer or to die," was the watchword between S. Teresa and her heavenly Spouse.

O Divine Spirit, how weak is man

unaided by Thee, but by Thy grace how strong he becomes. With Thee the cross is light, it is carried with gladness. If Thou art present nothing can disturb or affright us; the heart and tongue unite in singing Thy praises. If Thou hidest Thyself how feeble we become; the cross is unwelcome, and murmuringly taken up; every little trouble fills the heart with sadness, and gives rise to querulous repining.

Descend, O Spirit of Peace, Spirit of Gladness and of Might; descend into my heart, so that for the future I may love and esteem the cross more than I have hitherto shunned it. Give to me that I may find in suffering as much joy and delight as I have formerly found of bitterness. Endow me with so great a strength that the cross may not overwhelm me, but that I may patiently carry it with Jesus to the end of my life. Descend, then, O Mighty One, I beseech of Thee to come.

FIFTH MEDITATION.

On the Gift of Counsel.

The effects of the gift of Counsel are:
1. A discernment which enables us to distinguish between the movements of nature and of grace.
2. Submission to the interior drawing of the Holy Spirit.
3. Docility to the direction of the Holy Spirit.

FIRST POINT.

God only knows the full extent of man's blindness. We are continually walking in darkness, mistaking evil for good, and good for evil, and we are ever in danger of falling into error. The Sanctifier comes to our assistance, and bestows the gift of counsel.

1. By the light of counsel the soul is enabled to discern the source from which the impulses of the heart flow. It is a necessary and important light, it enables us to avoid the pitfalls of error. We murmur and fret over the faults of

our neighbour, and we imagine we are animated with a holy zeal. We fancy that it is lawful to retaliate injuries by stinging words, and we make ourselves believe we are acting in a prudent manner. We avoid those whose humour does not exactly harmonize with our own, and we call it discretion. We are guilty of tale-bearing, and to this we give the name of charity. So on with other things which we falsely regard as virtue, whereas, in truth, they spring from the natural movements of the heart. Through spiritual blindness we are for ever deceiving ourselves. A soul gifted with counsel sees all things in their true light; she is guided in the darkness, and by the aid of the Holy Spirit she clearly sees into the depths of her heart, and detects the snares which nature and the devil set to entrap unwary souls.

2. Besides this infused light, the Holy Ghost gives to the soul a strong interior impulse by which all natural inclinations are kept in subjection. Thus a great purity of heart is attained, for by the immediate suppression of all unlawful suggestions, imperfections are

kept at bay, and the soul begins to lead a life of holiness.

I confess, O Divine Spirit, that my eyes are held, and I cannot see into the depths of my own heart. The tempter has no need to arm himself against me, for I deceive myself and I am my own seducer. I mistake hastiness for zeal, evil inclinations for virtue. How hateful all this must be to Thy all-holy eyes! Stretch out Thy hand, I beseech Thee, and graciously give me sight.

SECOND POINT.

The second effect of the gift of counsel is submission to the interior drawing of the Holy Spirit. It is difficult to recognize the movements of nature, and immediately to suppress them; but it is a no less easy matter to discover and to follow the drawing of the Holy Ghost. For this end the gift of counsel is of absolute necessity. In what manner does the Holy Spirit work in the soul by this gift?

1. First, the Illuminator infuses into the soul a supernatural light, by which it is easy to ascertain from whence spring all interior impulses. By in-

spirations and whisperings the Holy Spirit speaks to the soul; these are, according to holy writ, His words and His voice. A child knows his father's voice, he can distinguish it amid a hundred other voices, and as soon as he hears it, the child runs towards his parent. Thus it is with the soul illuminated by the heavenly light; she recognizes the voice of the Holy Spirit. The devil, in vain, may seek to deceive her, but the gentle whispering of the Divine Counsellor cannot be mistaken.

2. Secondly, the Holy Spirit arouses in the heart such a tender love that the soul immediately hearkens to His voice. This is a great grace. Often it seems a hard matter to obey the inspirations of the Divine Guide; we are slow in following them; sometimes, indeed, we turn a deaf ear to the heavenly voice. The gifted soul hearkens instantly to the Beloved, and hastens to obey Him. Inflamed with love, she cries with the Spouse in the Canticles, "Behold, my Beloved speaketh to me: open to me, my sister, my love, my dove. My soul melted within me as He spoke."

It is thus Thou dost act, O Counsellor,

towards Thy faithful ones. Thou revealest to them Thy holy will, and at the same time Thou sweetly drawest them to its fulfilment. Have I not also a heart capable of loving Thee? How comes it, then, that I am so feebly moved by Thy gracious inspirations? Alas! I must weep over my insensibility. Thou standest at the gate, and I have not opened to Thee. Thou callest me, and I pay no heed to Thy voice. Thou revealest Thy will to me, and I do not fulfil it. All my misery is to be attributed to my own coldness.

THIRD POINT.

The continual guidance of the Sanctifier is most important to the soul. It is one of God's best gifts to man, it is conveyed to the soul through this gift. Obedience to this guidance is the third effect of counsel.

Consider, O my soul, the working of the Holy Spirit in this gift.

First, the Divine Guide governs and directs the affections. He makes His abode in the depths of the heart, breathing peace therein. As the soul is obedient to His voice, and watches for

His light, she is careful in repressing the impetuosity of nature. The Holy Spirit is enthroned as sovereign in the soul, and He takes delight in inundating her with spiritual sweetness, which lasts at times for days together.

Secondly, the Holy Spirit guides the exterior life. He treats the soul in the same manner as He treated the children of Israel in their wanderings through the desert. "He went before them to show the way, by day in a pillar of a cloud, and by night in a pillar of fire." The Holy Spirit infuses into the soul an inward light, by which she is able to see in what manner she should act, what is most perfect and pleasing in the sight of God.

Thirdly, the Holy Ghost guides the soul to holiness. Where He reigns as King there can be nothing done by halves. He excites to the practice of the most exalted virtue, and through His gracious assistance, what is naturally burdensome becomes light and easy. The soul gladly obeys the call of her Guide to the most menial works. No word of complaint escapes her in trying ills; nothing can ruffle her inward peace; she praises God unceasingly; and, after Christ's example, she returns good for evil, and loves even those who treat her ill.

O divine Spirit, how happy are those whom Thou dost deign to guide! To what heights of perfection may they not speedily attain, under Thy gracious direction. Why have I not given myself up to Thy guidance? Why have I been so slothful in following Thy inspirations? Had I been more diligent Thou wouldst now be reigning as King in my heart, and I should be walking in the footsteps of the Saints. The past has fled from me, I can but deplore my ill use of it. Yet all is not lost. Thy power and goodness, O adorable Spirit, are without measure; Thou canst and wilt assist me. Come, O Counsellor, come and take full possession of my whole being. Thou hast but to will it, and it will be done. Thy will is allpowerful. One spark is sufficient to enkindle Thy love within my heart, and to cause it to melt in sweet affection. Come, divine Spirit, I abandon myself without reserve into Thy holy hands. Do with me what Thou wilt; I have but one request to make of Thee, namely, that Thou wouldst make my heart fit to be directed by Thee. Guide me in all things, that I may know and do Thy Will. Strengthen me so powerfully that I may be able to suffer all that is inflicted on me, for love of Thee.

SIXTH MEDITATION.

On the Gift of Understanding.

The effects of the gift of Understanding are:
1. A capacity to apprehend the mysteries of Faith.
2. A firm belief in the truths of religion.
3. Conformity of heart to the dictates of Faith.

FIRST POINT.

The first effect of this gift is a capacity to apprehend what faith believes. All the faithful accept the same mysteries, but a vast difference exists between the belief of those who live simply according to the dictates of faith, and those who have been enlightened of the Holy Ghost, by means of the gift of understanding. For this gift gives a special intellectual power to understand with great clearness the truths of faith.

1. The light of faith is dim and obscure, the light of understanding is

bright and shining. There is the same difference between the two as there is between the light of a candle and the splendour of the sun at noon-day. Pictures in a room are indistinctly seen by the aid of a candle, but if the sunlight streams in all is different, and each picture is clearly seen in all its beauty of colour and outline.

Without an additional light from God, beyond the infused light of faith, the mysteries of religion would be but dimly discerned, they would make no great impression on the heart. The gift of understanding sanctifies the intellect, and is thus enabled to apprehend the things of faith with very clear spiritual vision. It is as if God partially drew aside the veil, and allowed us to gaze on the mysteries in the same manner as do the Saints in heaven.

2. If we only possess the light of faith, much meditation is requisite to the spiritual understanding of the doctrines of faith, but no sooner are we made partakers in this gift than all things become clear to us without effort or reflection on our part.

As we have seen by a comparison, it

is absolutely necessary to have the sunlight in order to see perfectly the pictures on a wall; so is it with the soul in regard to the ideas and knowledge of supernatural things. Faith sheds but a dim light, Understanding scatters the darkness, and opens the eye of the soul to spiritual knowing.

How desirable is this gift, O adorable Spirit, with what eagerness should I not covet it. Reason and will are closely knit; what is unknown of the one is unloved of the other. Without a share in this gift, I shall make no progress in virtue, my love will receive no increase. Teach me, O God, what it behoveth me to do, so as to obtain the gift of understanding.

SECOND POINT.

The light which radiates from the gift of understanding produces a twofold effect in the soul.

1. The first is a firmness of faith. This helps the soul to penetrate into hidden mysteries, and they seem so clear to her inward sight that she believes in them more readily than if she beheld them with bodily eyes. Reason

accepts them, believing in them steadfastly; for God reveals the truths of religion, which are so much beyond human knowledge, so clearly to the mind, that faith is no longer obscure, all is made bright and clear.

2. The second effect of this light is steadfastness in faith. Though the fiend may try, by his arts, to deceive the soul, laying snares for her by divers temptations, he could not cause her to fall or to doubt. If the world were to rise up against her, and she were threatened, like the martyrs of old, with torture and death, yet no victory could be gained over the steadfast soul. Like the mighty cedars of Libanus, which defy the tempest, the soul remains firmly rooted in her faith. "If all men were to change their religion," said a holy person, "and they were to do their utmost to try and shake my belief, they would gain nothing thereby. Methinks that I could conquer them through the power of faith, for it is so deeply fixed in my heart that hell itself could not shake it."

Knowledge so exalted, O divine Spirit, holds a mighty sway over the hearts of men, stirring them to despise all that is earthly. It gives strength to conquer temptations, and lends help in the trials of life. Unfortunately, I am little moved by the effects of this gift. I confess that until now I have made but little use of the light of faith, nor have I conformed my life to its principles, and this is the reason why still clearer light has not been vouchsafed to me.

THIRD POINT.

The third effect of the gift of understanding is conformity of heart to the dictates of faith. This working is greatly to be desired, for by it the heart is reformed, and all the affections are made holy, through the grace of the Holy Spirit. In order to understand this more thoroughly, it is well to ponder on the mysteries of faith, and then to consider what effect they have produced in the heart, comparing it with the effects which such considerations have wrought in the hearts of those endowed with understanding.

1. We believe that heaven is a place of eternal happiness, and we know that

the least portion of this bliss gives greater content to the soul than could the attainment of all worldly goods. But what impression does this revelation of faith make upon the hearts of the greater part of men? Scarcely any. They have but a feeble desire for their heavenly home, and they quit this life very reluctantly. These, however, are the sentiments only of those who are guided merely by the light of faith. Far otherwise is it with those who are illuminated by a more spiritual light, through the gift of understanding. The word heaven could not be pronounced in the hearing of S. Giles without his being ravished in ecstasy.

2. We believe also, that through love of man, Christ suffered His bitter death and Passion. Surely this thought should stir our hearts, and the knowledge of His sufferings should awaken loving pity within us. And yet it moves us little more than if our Blessed Lord were a stranger to us. It was not so with the Saints of God. Filled with the gift of the Holy Spirit, their feelings were stirred at this thought. The bare

mention of the name of Jesus Crucified caused S. Angela of Foligno to shed torrents of tears. So great was her love that she was rendered speechless through tender compassion for His sufferings.

How long, O Sanctifier, shall I remain with darkened intellect and unmoved heart? Wilt Thou not shed upon me one ray of that blessed light which Thou hast poured so freely upon Thy faithful servants? Give me, I pray Thee, a share in that love which was so overflowing in their hearts. It is not a mark of holiness to be filled with sensible devotion. The light of faith, I know, can lead me to holiness: but I am weak and I shall never be able to attain perfection unless Thou, O God, draw nigh to help me by special graces. Fill my understanding with Thy own light, so that I may be enabled to apprehend the wonders and the beauty hidden in Thy deep mysteries. Inflame my will with Thy divine love, that I may melt away in tenderness. Hearken unto my cry: not on account of my own merits, but according to Thy goodness and mercy, hear me. Hasten to come,

O Comforter, I know Thou canst not refuse to give to an orphaned soul that grace for which she yearns. Thou wilt not leave my heart in its arid state, Thou Who dost send down Thy refreshing showers so plentifully on the thirsty fields.

SEVENTH MEDITATION.

On the Gift of Wisdom.

The effects of the gift of Wisdom are:
1. Illumination in the intellect, by which we come to know God as far as it is possible to man in this life.
2. A tender love of God.
3. Complete change of heart, by which we are reformed to the likeness of God.

FIRST POINT.

The gift of wisdom is the last and crowning gift of the Holy Ghost. It makes us happy in this life by knitting us in close communion with God. Wisdom is a spiritual light infused by the Uncreated Spirit into the soul of man. It leads us to God, and by its brightness we are helped to see and know Him in His divine perfection. Consider now, O my soul, the excellent qualities of this admirable light.

1. First, by the light of wisdom we

are helped to know God as far as it is possible to us to know Him in this life. The soul adorned with wisdom is like unto one who receives the gift of sight in middle age. What notion, think you, could such a one have formed of the world during the years he was deprived of sight? He believed in the existence of the sun and of the heavenly bodies; he knew that the earth brings forth fruit and flowers, that fish swim in the waters, that birds fly in the air, and that on the earth dwell divers kinds of beasts. He believed all this on the assurance of others, but because these things were held from his sight he took no joy in their being. But what would be his astonishment, his enraptured delight, when suddenly his eyes were opened, and for the first time he beholds the splendour of the sun, the green-clad mountains, the fruit-laden trees, and the flowery meadows? With what ravishment would he not gaze on nature's beauty?

Compare this with a soul who possesses only the light of faith. She believes God to be the essence of perfection; she knows that He is infinite goodness, beauty, and power. But as the light by which she discerns these things is of itself too dim, she is excited neither to great love nor gladness by her knowledge of God's perfection. A marvellous change is wrought in this soul as soon as the Holy Ghost bestows on her the gift of wisdom. Then do the perfections of the Godhead shine forth on her spiritual vision in all their excellence, and by the contemplation thereof she is powerfully allured to the love of God. She is, as it were, beside herself, and in her bewilderment she feels herself to be submerged in the shoreless sea of God's perfection.

2. Secondly, by the aid of the light of wisdom we not only come to know God, but we taste and enjoy Him with an exceeding contentment.

"It is one thing," says S. Bonaventure, "to know that honey is sweet, and another to realize its sweetness by the taste." We know by faith that God is wonderfully good, but it is only after we have been illuminated by the light of wisdom that we are able to discern His exceeding goodness. The heart is then filled to overflowing, and the soul tastes how sweet God is. Wisdom was the source of the saints' great love of prayer. "O Brother," cried S. Francis Borgia, to one who broke in upon his recollection, "leave me at least for a quarter of an hour to enjoy my happiness."

Who will give me a fountain of tears, that I may weep over my past folly? Thou, O Divine Spirit, art generous and merciful to the clean of heart. It is only needful to be detached from creatures in order to be allowed to repose on Thy adorable bosom, and by detachment we draw down the dew of heaven into our hearts. I bewail my foolishness in setting my affections on those things which could never fill me with contentment.

SECOND POINT.

The tender love which the Holy Ghost infuses into the heart through the gift of wisdom has two properties which clearly prove the excellence of this gift.

1. The first property of this love is fervour. It is not merely a love of predilection, which may take its rise from the light of faith, but it is like unto a

flame which penetrates into the very marrow of the soul, filling it with grace and spiritual sweetness. It wasteth the heart, and consumeth all its affections in God. The soul thus gathered up into Him does not pour herself forth in loving words or sighs, but simply melts away, as it were, in love.

Armelle thus describes this happy state: "I spent my leisure moments in a retired place, not in formal prayer, for the greater part of the time I gave no thought to it. I threw myself in loving transport in the arms of Him who is my love and my all. I held Him in close embrace, praising and blessing His holy name, while my whole being melted in the fire of love and gratitude. Love consumed me, I felt beside myself, and it was with difficulty I could contain my joy. Then did my Beloved lovingly caress me, and in the ravishment of love we were so united that we became both one."

2. The second property of this love is constancy. Walking in the gift of wisdom, the soul becomes so united with God that she easily maintains a spiritual consciousness of His abiding presence.

A constant habit of recollection is with very great difficulty attained by one who is guided only by faith.

"God," again says the Blessed Armelle, "never hid Himself from my eyes, nor did He ever close the gate of His mercy on me. If He withdrew Himself somewhat, it was but momentarily, and immediately after He bestowed on me still greater marks of love and friendship. For my part, my soul and all its desires were wholly fixed on Him; He was my only Love." Who would not yearn for this treasure of wisdom? To know Thee, O Uncreated Spirit, to love Thee, and to think of Thee, form all the true happiness of man. Did our Lord not say, "The kingdom of God is within you"? If, then, we may find Him present within, here we can embrace Him, and sweetly repose in Him. Lift thyself up, O my soul, and breathe forth thy sighs to thy God, who is generous exceedingly.

THIRD POINT.

The third effect of wisdom is a complete change of heart, by which we are reformed into the likeness of God. In this transformation of the soul lies the principal operation and end of this gift. "Wisdom," says Gerson, "consists in a union of love between God and the soul; by it the latter is transformed into His likeness." What, then, are the chief means by which the Divine Sanctifier effects this transformation?

1. The first is an annihilation of all purely natural propensions and affections. The pure and burning love which the Holy Ghost breathes into the soul destroys all the inclinations of our fleshy nature, and it lifts her above the things of earth, wooing her to love of God alone. Love of Him then reigns supreme, and creatures are loved only for His sake. In the honour and glory of God the soul takes all her joy, and she is grieved only at the sight of sin. She yearns for greater love of God, she is stirred to suffer and to work for Him.

2. The second means by which the Holy Ghost effects this transmutation is by filling the soul with a rest and quietness in all her inward powers. This tranquillity is the fruit of love, the working of the Spirit of God. In tak-

ing up His abiding-place in a soul, He enters as king and guide; He really becomes the director of her interior life.

The light infused by the Holy Ghost into the memory, intellect, and will, enables the soul to think continually of God, to see His perfection ever more clearly, and causes her to burn with renewed fire of love. The Sanctifier likewise directs the external life, for by degrees He guides the soul to choose the most perfect way, showing her by His light what is well-pleasing to Himself. Thus the soul is led in all things by the Divine Guide, and her life becomes all-holy.

My conscience whispers to me that it is an exceeding boldness on my part even to desire this heavenly gift. O Giver of Wisdom, my heart is as yet unprepared for so great a grace. I have done nothing to draw it into my soul. I rely on Thy goodness, and trusting to Thy mercy I send forth my sighs to Thee.

Come, O Sanctifier, and accomplish the desires of my heart. The more generous Thy gifts, the more fervently Thou wilt be loved and honoured. My heart has been as dry and arid as the land on which no rain has fallen; but if Thou wilt deign to visit it all will be refreshed, and it will melt away in the tenderness of love. Descend, I implore of Thee, O Divine Spirit.

www.ingramcontent.com/pod-product-compliance
Lightning Source LLC
Chambersburg PA
CBHW020246090426

42735CB00010B/1858